Old Songs

OLGA SEDAKOVA

Old Songs

1980–1981

Translated by
Martha M. F. Kelly

Foreword by
Rowan Williams

SL/.NT
BOOKS

OLD SONGS

Slant Books
P.O. Box 60295
Seattle, WA 98160

www.slantbooks.org

Cataloguing-in-Publication data:

Names: Sedakova, Olga.

Title: Old songs / Olga Sedakova.

Description: Seattle, WA: Slant Books, 2023

Identifiers: ISBN 978-1-63982-142-6 (hardcover) |ISBN 978-1-63982-141-9 (paperback) | ISBN 978-1-63982-142-6 (ebook)

Subjects: LCSH: Russian poetry | Russian poetry--20th century--Translations into English | Sedakova, Ol'ga | Folk poetry, Russian

Contents

Foreword

OLGA SEDAKOVA IS WITHOUT doubt one of the foremost Russian poets of her generation—an unusual generation, whose writing spans the end of the repressions of the Soviet era and the beginnings of a new age of angry, violent nationalism, often clothed in religious dress. Her detachment from these varieties of anti-humanism is consistent and deep; her Christian imagination is strong enough never to be simply reactive, nostalgic, or resentful. Like any good poet, she is most concerned with making the reader *attend*, both to the patterning and pacing of her words and to what they illuminate about being alive in the world. If there is, for her, a "consolation" in poetry, it is not a matter of simple aesthetic satisfaction or of encouraging "messages." She sees her words as drawing us into a journey in which we shall certainly get lost. In our lostness, we may just become able to glimpse, in a sky or a mirror or a patch of grass on a hillside or a stray sound, the pressure all around us of immeasurable joy, a joy that does not need us and our feelings for it to be real.

Mirrors turn up often in these poems, with the subtext of reminding us of the difficulties we have in seeing ourselves, the enormous gaps in our knowledge of who and what we are; we need all sorts of accompaniment if we are to see our own faces with any kind of truthfulness. And—to pick up a resonant turn of phrase from one of these poems—part of what makes it impossible for Adam, even a penitent Adam, to get back into the Garden of Eden is that he has "wanted" what is already his—he has tried to grasp and possess his own being and that of his world, instead of journeying into himself and the world, journeying into language itself, so as to become more attuned to truth, and so to joy.

The poems in this volume are different from many of those that have appeared in earlier translations. Sedakova often writes with a long, "drifting" line, fingering over an image or a sequence of words interspersed with shorter, more insistent lines. Her vocabulary can be difficult, sometimes archaic. But these pieces are tightly constructed, with plenty of balladic energy and folkloric pithiness, even when their content is teasing and complex. They very definitely succeed in conveying the sense of a forgotten directness of perception and relation—not a lost simplicity, exactly, but a larger and more human world shrunk and damaged by "adult" modernity. The way back is never the reconstruction of a lost golden age, but a new willingness to let go in the face of the pinpoint of luminosity that is still a gateway to life, to see that we can't see who we are in our habitual ways of thinking. It is the simplicity and the superabundance of life in grace.

She is seldom an easy poet and putting her into English is hard work (my own efforts at this have sometimes left me feeling that every kind of verbal grace has vanished in the process); it is excellent that she has found here such a careful, skilled, and sympathetic translator. Sedakova is someone who, as both a poet and critic, deserves to be much better known in the English-speaking world—and just at present it is extremely important that we recognize the strain in Russian culture that is deeply subversive of the imperial and totalizing ambitions that continue to distort a great heritage of wisdom and imagination. Olga Sedakova is a writer of global significance, a premier voice of Christian humanism and sacramental sensibility, and the publishing of this collection is a welcome stage in the reception of her exceptional genius in the West.

—Rowan Williams

Translator's Introduction

ON DECEMBER 7, 2016, Olga Sedakova joined Svetlana Aleksievich's "Intellectual Club" as its inaugural guest. Aleksievich, the Nobel Prize-winning author, introduced Sedakova, saying, "When you read her poetry, it's as though you walk out into a summer garden and suddenly you see that you're alive." When you read her, she continued, you understand you are not alone—that, indeed, you are surrounded by people who have shown you how to live with courage in and through a community of interlocutors. Sedakova then spoke about traditional Russian notions of evil. How, she asked, can so many Russians praise the genocidal Soviet dictator Joseph Stalin as having done what was necessary to win a world war? Russia needs two things, Sedakova said. It needs better tools for discerning good from evil, and it needs a "culture of discussion" so people can learn to discern together.

Sedakova emerged as a poet in the mid-1970s when Leonid Brezhnev headed the Soviet Communist Party. By that era of "Stagnation," people were no longer executed for speaking out; but frank discussion took place only in relatively sheltered circles—around the kitchen table, as people liked to say. For many, it was a time of hopelessness and suffocation, a time when alcohol was a common escape, when social and political ideals seemed abused beyond repair. Into this context spoke a tender voice with uncommon authority, a voice that makes a crowded room go quiet and everyone and everything lean in to hear language made new with trust and vulnerable hope.

People sometimes describe Sedakova as a "difficult" poet. There is no denying her erudition: she is one of a historic handful of Russian-language metaphysical poets, and she is a renowned scholar and translator. She is also part of a generation whose art reflects a "longing for world culture" reaching beyond the confines of their Soviet context.[1] Some of Sedakova's books of poetry advertise her ongoing dialogue with European and classical Chinese poetry and philosophy, such as *A Chinese Journey* (*Kitaiskoe puteshestvie*, 1986) with its epigraph from Lao Tse or *Stanzas in the Manner of Alexander Pope* (*Stansy v manere Aleksandra Popa*, 1979-80).

And then there are her images, which can defy conventional physics. In one poem from *Old Songs,* the speaker muses,

> I mean, life is such a small thing:
> it can pull its whole self together
> on your pinkie, on the tip of your eyelash.
> And death surrounds it like the sea.

If *Old Songs* are "difficult," it is likely because we, her contemporary readers, struggle with their logic of the fairytale and the parable or with the poems' unapologetically paradoxical proclamations. Sedakova wrote these verses in an era that viewed the Communist Revolution as having achieved the razing of bourgeois culture and economics to construct a new, socialist society with a new Soviet man and Soviet woman. Sedakova's *Old Songs* resist this straight, ascendant line into the future. In one poem, the speaker says to the "Word" of its title ("Slovo"),

> These eyes of ours can never see
> your truest, deepest color,
> no human ear can ever hear
> the rustle of your broad, broad folds.

The poetic word conceals in its folds the secrets of the cosmos and the wisdom of the ages. Hence also the constant presence of Sedakova's beloved grandmother in this volume. It was she who first shaped the poet's Orthodox Christian faith—not as a national identity, but as a way of perceiving and relating to the world, a mode marked by delight and deep attention.

Olga Aleksandrovna Sedakova was born in Moscow on December 26, 1949, into the family of a Soviet military engineer and thus into a family of some status. As a child, she published early verses in a Communist youth magazine. But once in college, at Moscow State University, she entered the artistic and intellectual Underground, developing close friendships with some of its most famous figures, such as Venedikt Erofeev, author of the virtuosically intoxicated *Moscow to the End of the Line* (*Moskva-Petushki*), and scholar Sergei Averintsev, who drew many hundreds to his semi-public lectures on Byzantine Christianity.

Sedakova went on to study not only philology but also ethnography, achieving the prestigious Candidate of Sciences title with a dissertation on the burial rites of the eastern and southern Slavs, which she defended in 1984. Written from 1980-81, *Old Songs* betrays more than a scholarly interest in folk wisdom. The following year, in 1982, Sedakova penned a poetic memoir in which ethnographic interest bleeds into a literary metaphysics. Entitled "Notes on and Recollections of Various Poems, and Also, In Praise of Poetry," the piece recounts Sedakova's life through her encounters with poetry. The events are internal and described as world-altering sensation. A key passage describes the moment Sedakova received her poetic calling at age fifteen. She and two high school friends travel to a village to see in the New Year. They make preparations for Christmas Eve divinations (January 6, by the traditional calendar).

> But the old woman next door had filled our heads with such frightening stories about divination that by midnight we were afraid even to step on the floor, much less to tell fortunes . . . I cowered on top of the stove, rigid with fear. And this is when the happening happened. I could not grasp what was taking place then, nor can I now. And thus, I am unable to lay it all out in a comprehensible manner. But auditory or visual hallucination played no role here. What did play a role was something inside me. Here is the most intelligible way I can describe it: the stove turned out to be the center of the world, and this center was hurtling forward to someplace, or maybe, in fact, everything was hurtling past it. And this was not a sensation—it was an actual event: its reality did not depend on whether I sensed it or not, much as an incident out in the street does not.[2]

While Sedakova pokes light fun at her vision, the gripping image of the quantum rustic village stove projects an imaginary shaped by oral culture and modern learning alike.

For decades Sedakova's poems were published only in samizdat—"self-published" formats copied by hand or typewriter and distributed amongst circles of trust and relative secrecy. Her readings took place in private apartments or art studios. An old friend of hers, literary scholar Irina Surat, recalls first attending one such reading: "I can say without exaggeration that it was stunning. It simply bowled me over, that reading. It was magic—that's how it felt to me. Not a subject of philological interest but a phenomenon that was really and truly magical. That transfigures you and carries you away somewhere. It was the sensation of another world."[3]

Since the collapse of the Soviet Union in 1991, Sedakova has written less poetry. But she has written more and more essays and cultural criticism. And she has never stopped translating. Common themes emerge across her prose, most prominently the need for more refined moral judgment and the related quest to reconstitute Russia's social fabric. With her many national and international recognitions, including a prize awarded by Pope John Paul II, she is known as one of Russia's greatest living poets. Indeed, few of her generation are left—in Russia and beyond. The role of Russian poet is freighted with expectations. Iconic nineteenth-century poet Alexander Pushkin cemented a construct of the poet as one who speaks eternal truth when political repression and heavy censorship shut other mouths. He died in a duel at age 37 and was buried in secret by dark of night because the regime feared mass gatherings at a public funeral.

Sedakova not only speaks of the fearsome responsibility of the poet but has put herself at risk more than once—by signing a public declaration, in 2014, against the invasion of the Crimea, by writing a piece that went viral, critiquing Russian civil society negatively in the light of the Maidan uprisings in Ukraine. As I write this, she is hunkered down in Moscow, having decided to stay for now. She is horrified by what her country is doing to a nation some of her oldest friends and closest collaborators call home.

Sedakova is a revered figure in Russia—at least for those who value literature and intellect in the public arena. Some of her poetry hits a high, even odic, register that accords to the image of the learned, solemn voice of conscience. *Old Songs,* on the other hand, hits notes of humble knowing. I have, by now, translated a good deal of Sedakova's poetry. And as difficult as it can be to translate her more high-faluting works—with their classical structures, literary and philosophical allusions, and their refined diction—it is perhaps more challenging to translate poems like the ones in this volume.

The Russian of *Old Songs* draws heavily on Russian oral cultures. Think of your grandmother (or your great-grandmother, if you knew her—or your friend's grandmother) and her turns of phrase. Our family returns to a whole stock of these from my North Carolina grandmother, who grew up in a small rural town. "They say it takes a smart one to play the fool." "He's tighter than Dick's hat band." "That's pure-tee meanness." How would you, pray tell, translate these into Russian—especially when there is no real corresponding phrase?

The work of this translation has been to convey a sense of words worn down smooth as a river rock, handled for generations by passing currents, maybe grasped in a coat pocket to recall peaceful, shimmering summer days by the water. I have aimed to be as faithful as possible to Sedakova's words and images. But over multiple iterations, I have polished away what I could, trying as deftly as possible to add small echoes of something like oral tradition in English—here a bit of fairy tale or nursery rhyme, there an aphoristic turn. Sedakova's accentual meter helps, with its regular beats but variable number of syllables. Folk songs and pop songs use such meter to keep time while using as few or as many words as they want. (Think Joni Mitchell.) I have tried to maintain that same pulse and freedom here.

Reading in English, you and I cannot access the particular "oldness" Sedakova references. But as Eric Hobsbawm and others remind us, tradition is ever new, always being reinvented.[4] This was as true when Sedakova wrote these verses into a late Soviet urban space as it is sending out an English version of them in 2022, with Russia destroying Ukrainian infrastructure as winter approaches to make up for its failures on the battlefield. May you find something "old" here that feels sustaining, or, on the other hand, like a pebble in your shoe. (The voice here does not necessarily mind telling you how things are, even when it escapes rational logic.) Sedakova is, after all, a student of the "Perennial Tradition," which seeks in diverse ways to address contemporaneity as the eternal novice it is.

December 2022
Research Triangle Park, North Carolina

Endnotes

1. Osip Mandelstam used this phrase in 1933 to describe the Russian Acmeist school of poetry, most active in the 1910s and '20s (O. Mandel'shtam, *Slovo i kul'tura* [Moscow: Sov'etskii Pisatel', 1987], 298). Later, writers of the late Soviet Underground adopted the phrase as a kind of motto.

2. Translation by the author. Readers can find a full translation of this seminal, autobiographical essay in Olga Sedakova, *In Praise of Poetry*, ed. Caroline Clark, Ksenia Golubovich and Stephanie Sandler (Open Letter, 2014). The volume also contains Stephanie Sandler's wonderful translation of *Old Songs*.

3. Irina Surat, unpublished interview, October 16, 2017.

4. Eric Hobsbawm, *The Invention of Tradition* (Cambridge: Cambridge University Press, 1983).

Old Songs

ПЕРВАЯ ТЕТРАДЬ

Что белеется на горе зеленой?

А.С. Пушкин

1. ОБИДА

Что же ты, злая обида?
я усну, а ты не засыпаешь,
я проснусь, а ты давно проснулась
и смотришь на меня, как гадалка.

Или скажешь, кто меня обидел?
Нет таких, над всеми Бог единый.
Кому нужно—дает Он волю,
у кого не нужно—отбирает.

Или жизнь меня не полюбила?
Ах, неправда, любит и жалеет,
бережет в потаенном месте
и достанет, только пожелает,
поглядит, как никто не умеет.

Что же ты, злая обида,
сидишь предо мной, как гадалка?

Или скажешь, что живу я плохо,
обижаю больных и несчастных....

FIRST NOTEBOOK

What gleams white there on the green hill?

—A.S. Pushkin

1. GRUDGE

What's this, then, bitter grudge?
I nod off, but you won't go to sleep,
I wake up, there you are, long awake
watching me like a fortuneteller.

What, has somebody done me wrong?
Not a soul, there's one God over all.
He gives freedom to those who need it,
and from those who don't—he takes it away.

What, has life not loved me enough?
Ah, not true, it loves me, feels sorry for me,
it shelters me in a quiet place,
comes and gets me whenever it likes,
looks at me like nobody else does.

What's this, then, bitter grudge?
There you sit like a fortuneteller.

What, you say that I live badly,
doing ill to the sick and unhappy? ...

2. КОНЬ

Едет путник по темной дороге,
не торопится, едет и едет.

—Спрашивай, конь, меня что хочешь,
всё спроси—я всё тебе отвечу.
Люди меня слушать не будут,
Бог и без рассказов знает.

Странное, странное дело,
почему огонь горит на свете,
почему мы полночи боимся
и бывает ли кто счастливым?

Я скажу, а ты не поверишь,
как люблю я ночь и дорогу,
как люблю я, что меня прогнали
и что завтра опять прогонят.

Подойди, милосердное время,
выпей моей юности похмелье,
вытяни молодости жало
из недавней горячей ранки—
и я буду умней, чем другие!

Конь не говорит, а отвечает,
тянется долгая дорога.
И никто не бывает счастливым.
Но несчастных тоже немного.

2. STEED

The wayfarer rides and rides
down the dark road, and he never hurries.

"Ask me, steed, whatever you want,
whatever you ask, I'll answer.
It's not like people listen to me,
and God doesn't need my stories to know.

"It is a strange, strange thing,
why does fire burn on earth,
why are we afraid of midnight,
and is anyone out there happy?

"I'll tell you, but you won't believe me,
how I love the night and the road,
how I love how they drove me off,
how they'll do it again tomorrow.

"Come forth, oh, time of mercy,
drink down the hops of my youth,
pull out the sting of childhood
from the burning hot fresh wound—
make me cleverer than all the rest!"

The steed answers without saying a word,
and the long road stretches out.
And there's not a soul who is happy.
But not many are unhappy either.

3. СУДЬБА

Кто же знает, что ему судили?
Кто и угадает—не заметит.

Может, и ты меня вспомнишь,
когда я про тебя забуду.

И тогда я войду неслышно,
как к живым приходят неживые,
и скажу, что кое-что знаю,
чего ты никогда не узнаешь.

А потом поцелую руку,
как холопы господам целуют.

3. FATE

Who knows what fate he's been dealt?
The one who guessed it would never say.

And maybe one day you'll remember me
when I've gone and forgotten you.

And then I'll enter without a sound,
as the dead come to see the living,
and I'll tell you that I know something,
something you'll never find out.

And then I will kiss your hand
as serfs do with their lords.

4. ДЕТСТВО

Помню я раннее детство
и сон в золотой постели.

Кажется или правда? —
кто-то меня увидел,
быстро вошел из сада
и стоит улыбаясь.

—Мир—говорит,—пустыня.
Сердце человека—камень.
Любят люди, чего не знают.

Ты не забудь меня, Ольга,
а я никого не забуду.

4. CHILDHOOD

I remember early childhood
and my dream in the golden bed.

Was it real, or just a dream?—
someone caught sight of me,
he rushed in from the garden
and he just stood there, smiling.

"The world," he said, "is a wilderness.
The human heart is a stone.
People love what they don't know.

"Don't you forget me, Olga;
as for me, I won't forget a soul."

5. ГРЕХ

Можно обмануть высокое небо—
высокое небо всего не увидит.
Можно обмануть глубокую землю—
глубокая земля спит и не слышит.
Ясновидцев, гадателей и гадалок—
а себя самого не обманешь.

Ох, не любят грешного человека
зеркала, и стёкла, и вода лесная:
там чужая кровь то бежит, как ветер,
то свернется, как змея больная:

—Завтра мы встанем пораньше
и пойдем к знаменитой гадалке,
дадим ей за работу денег,
чтобы она сказала,
что ничего не видит.

5. SIN

You can fool the high, high sky—
the high, high sky can't see everything.
You can fool the deep, deep earth—
the deep, deep earth is asleep and can't hear.
Clairvoyants and fortunetellers, too—
but yourself, you'll never fool.

Ah, mirrors, windows, and forest water
have no love for the sinful man:
in them foreign blood runs like wind one minute
then twists like a sick snake the next:

"Tomorrow, we'll get up early
and go see the famed fortuneteller,
we'll pay a tidy sum
to have her say to us
that she can't see a thing."

6.

Человек он злой и недобрый,
скверный человек и несчастный.
И кажется, мне его жалко,
а сама я еще недобрее.

И когда мы с ним говорили,
давно и не помню сколько,
ночь была и дождь не кончался,
будто бы что задумал,
будто кто-то спускался
и шел в слезах и сам как слезы:

не о себе, не о небе,
не о лестнице длинной,
не о том, что было,
не о том, что будет,—

ничего не будет.
Ничего не бывает.

6.

There's a man who is spiteful and mean,
a bad man and unhappy too.
Somehow, I feel sorry for him,
though I'm even more unkind.

And when we talked, the two of us—
how long ago, I couldn't say—
it was late at night, and the rain wouldn't stop,
as though it was thinking of something,
as though there was someone coming down
in tears, someone who was very like tears:

not for himself or the sky,
not for the long, long staircase,
not for what has been,
and not for what will be—

for there's not a thing that will be.
There's not a thing that is.

7. УТЕШЕНЬЕ

Не гадай о собственной смерти
и не радуйся, что все пропало,
не задумывай, как тебя оплачут,
как замучит их поздняя жалость.

Это всё плохое утешенье,
для земли обидная забава.

Лучше скажи и подумай:
что белеет на горе зеленой?

На горе зеленой сады играют
и до самой воды доходят,
как ягнята с золотыми бубенцами.
Белые ягнята на горе зеленой.

А смерть придет, никого не спросит.

7. CONSOLATION

Don't try to foretell your own death
and don't rejoice when all is lost,
don't imagine how they'll grieve for you,
or how belated pity will torment them.

All of that's cold comfort,
a game that's hurtful to the earth.

Better instead to wonder aloud:
what gleams white there on the green hill?

On the green hill gardens play,
they go right up to the water's edge
like lambs with golden bells.
White lambs on a green, green hill.

For death will come, will ask no one.

8. СПОР

Разве мало я живу на свете?
Страшно и выговорить, сколько.
А всё себя сердце не любит.
Ходит, как узник по темнице,—
а в окне чего только не видно!

Вот одна старуха говорила:
—Хорошо, тепло в Божьем мире.
Как горошины в гороховых лопатках,
лежим мы в ладони Господней.
И кого ты просишь—не вернется.
И чего ни задумай—не исполнишь.
А порадуется этому сердце,
будто птице в узорную клетку
бросили сладкие зерна—
тоже ведь подарок не напрасный!

Я кивнула, а в уме сказала:
Помолчи ты, глупая старуха.
Всё бывает, и больше бывает.

8. OBJECTION

How long have I lived on this earth?
I hesitate even to say.
And still the heart won't love itself.
It paces its cell like a prisoner—
while out the window there's a world to see!

There was an old woman who said,
"It's good and warm on God's green earth.
Like peas cradled in their pods,
we curl up in God's palms.
Who's asked a favor will never come back.
And what's dreamed up will never come true.
Still, the heart takes joy in all of this,
like sweet, sweet seeds that someone throws
to a bird in an ornate cage—
even that small gift has meaning."

I nodded, but in my mind, I said,
"Be quiet, you stupid old woman.
There's more than you know that goes on."

9. ПРОСЬБА

Бедные, бедные люди!
И не злы они, а торопливы:
хлеб едят—и больше голодают,
пьют—и от вина трезвеют.

Если бы меня спросили,
я бы сказала: Боже,
сделай меня чем-нибудь новым!

Я люблю великое чудо
и не люблю несчастья.

Сделай, как камень отграненный,
и потеряй из перстня
на песке пустыни.

Чтобы лежал он тихо,
не внутри, не снаружи,
а повсюду, как тайна.

И никто бы его не видел,
только свет внутри и свет снаружи.

А свет играет, как дети,
малые дети и ручные звери.

9. REQUEST

Oh, these poor, poor people!
It's not that they're bad; they're just hurried:
eating their bread leaves them hungrier,
and a drink—even wine—leaves them sober.

Ask me,
and I'll say, "Oh, God,
make of me something new!"

I love great signs and wonders,
and I don't love unhappiness.

Change me into a cut gem,
and lose me from your ring
in the desert sand.

And let it lie there in peace,
not inwardly or outwardly,
but everywhere, like a mystery.

And no one would ever see it,
just the light inside and the light outside.

And the light, it plays like children,
wee children and tame beasts.

10. СЛОВО

И кто любит, того полюбят.
Кто служит, тому послужат—
не теперь, так когда-нибудь после.

Но лучше тому, кто благодарен,
кто пойдет, послужив, без Рахили
веселый, по холмам зеленым.

Ты же, слово, царская одежда,
долгого, короткого терпенья платье,
выше неба, веселее солнца.

Наши глаза не увидят
цвета твоего родного,
шума складок твоих широких
не услышат уши человека,

только сердце само себе скажет:
—Вы свободны, и будете свободны,
и перед рабами не в ответе.

1980

10. WORD

And the one who loves will be loved.
The one who serves will be served—
if not now, then some other time.

But it's better yet to be grateful,
to serve and set out without Rachel,
in good cheer down along the green hills.

And you, oh word, are the clothes of a king,
a robe of patience, long and short,
you're higher yet than the sky
and more cheerful yet than the sun.

These eyes of ours can never see
your truest, deepest color,
no human ear can ever hear
the rustle of your broad, broad folds.

The heart, though, will say to itself,
"You are free, and you shall be free,
you don't have to answer to those still enslaved."

1980

ВТОРАЯ ТЕТРАДЬ

Посвящается бабушке

1. СМЕЛОСТЬ И МИЛОСТЬ

Солнце светит на правых и неправых,
и земля нигде себя не хуже:
хочешь, иди на восток, на запад
или куда тебе скажут,
хочешь—дома оставайся.

Смелость правит кораблями
на океане великом.
Милость качает разум,
как глубокую дряхлую люльку.

Кто знает смелость, знает и милость,
потому что они—как сестры:
смелость легче всего на свете,
легче всех дел—милосердье.

SECOND NOTEBOOK

Dedicated to my grandmother

1. BOLDNESS AND MERCY

The sun shines on the just and the unjust too,
and there's nowhere on earth worse than anywhere else:
go east or go west, wherever you like,
or wherever they tell you to go,
or if you like—just stay home.

It's boldness that pilots ships
on the great and mighty ocean.
And it's mercy that rocks our reason to sleep
like a deep and age-old cradle.

If you know boldness, you know mercy too,
because they are like sisters:
boldness is lighter than all things on earth,
but compassion is lighter than anything.

2. ПОХОДНАЯ ПЕСНЯ

Во Францию два гренадера из русского плена брели.
В пыли их походное платье, и Франция тоже в пыли.

Не правда ли, странное дело? Вдруг жизнь оседает,
                                                 как прах,
как снег на смоленских дорогах,
                          как песок в аравийских степях.

И видно далёко, далёко, и небо виднее всего.
—Чего же Ты, Господи, хочешь,
                          чего ждешь от раба Твоего?

Над всем, чего мы захотели, гуляет какая-то плеть.
Глаза бы мои не глядели. Да велено, видно, глядеть.

И ладно. Чего не бывает над смирной и грубой землей?
В какой высоте не играет кометы огонь роковой?

Вставай же, товарищ убогий! Солдатам валяться не след.
Мы выпьем за верность до гроба:
                          за гробом неверности нет.

2. A MARCHING SONG

Two grenadiers went wandering to France from their Russian captivity.
Their travel garb was covered in dust, and France was dusty too.

It's a strange thing, don't you agree? How life goes suddenly grey
                                            as ash,
as snow on the Smolensk roads,
                       as sand on the Arabian steppes.

And you can see so far, so far, and you can see the sky best of all.
"Well then, Lord, what do You want,
                       what would You ask of Your servant?

"Over everything that we've desired dangles something like a whip.
My eyes would look the other way, but we're bidden, it seems, to look.

"Well, that's alright. All kinds of things go on above our serene, crude earth.
Is there any height where the comet's fatal fire does not play?

"Get up, then, wretched comrade mine! A soldier should never wallow.
Raise a glass to loyalty unto the grave:
                       there's no disloyalty beyond."

3. НЕВЕРНАЯ ЖЕНА

С того дня, как ты домой вернулся
и на меня не смотришь,
все во мне переменилось.

Как та вон больная собака
третий день лежит, издыхает,
так и душа моя ноет.

Грешному весь мир заступник,
а невинному—только чудо.
Пусть мне чудо и будет свидетель.

Покажи ему, Боже, правду,
покажи мое оправданье!—

Тут собака, бедное созданье,
быстро головой тряхнула,
весело к ней подбежала,
ласково лизнула руку—
и упала мертвая на землю.

Знает Бог о человеке,
чего человек не знает.

3. THE UNFAITHFUL WIFE

Ever since you came back home
you won't even look at me,
and everything in me has changed.

Like that sick dog who's been lying there
dying for three days now,
my soul just won't stop aching.

The whole world pleads for the sinful
while the innocent's saved by a miracle alone.
May a miracle, then, be my witness.

Show him the truth, oh, God,
show him my innocence!—

And at that the dog, poor creature,
briskly shook its head,
friskily ran up to her,
affectionately licked her hand—
and fell down dead on the ground.

God knows things a person
doesn't know about himself.

4. УВЕРЕНИЕ

Хоть и все над тобой посмеются,
и будешь ты лежать, как Лазарь,
лежать и молчать перед небом—
и тогда ты Лазарем не будешь.

Ах, хорошо сравняться
с черной землей садовой,
с пестрой придорожной пылью,

с криком малого ребенка,
которого в поле забыли . . .

а другого у тебя не просят.

4. ASSURANCE

Even if everyone laughs at you
as you lie there like Lazarus,
lie wordless before heaven,—
it doesn't make you Lazarus.

Why would you want to compete
with the black earth of the garden,
with the littered roadside dust,

with the cry of a tiny child
abandoned out in the field . . .

for nothing more will be asked of you.

5. КОЛЫБЕЛЬНАЯ

На горе, в урочище еловом,
на тонкой высокой макушке
подвязана колыбелка.

Ветер ее качает.

Вместе с колыбелкой—клетку,
с клеткой—дуплистую елку.

В клетке разумная птица
свистит и горит, как свечка.

—Спи,—говорит,—голубчик,
кем захочешь, тем и проснешься:
хочешь, бедным, хочешь, богатым,
хочешь—морской волной,
хочешь—ангелом Господним.

5. CRADLE SONG

High on a hill in a stand of firs,
up on its narrow crown
a little cradle is strung.

And the wind does rock it.

And with the cradle, there's a cage,
and with the cage, a hollow fir.

There in the cage, a sagacious bird
whistles and burns like a candle.

"Sleep," it says, "my little dove,
when you wake, you'll be whoever you wish:
rich, if you wish; poor, if you wish;
if you wish—a wave of the sea;
if you wish—an angel of the Lord."

6. ВОЗВРАЩЕНИЕ

Стих об Алексее

Хорошо куда-нибудь вернуться:
в город, где всё по-другому,
в сад, где иные деревья
давно срубили, остальные
скрипят, а раньше не скрипели,
в дом, где по тебе горюют.

Вернуться и не назваться.
Так и молчать до смерти.

Пусть они себе гадают,
расспрашивают приезжих,
понимают—и не понимают.

А вещи кругом сияют,
как далекие мелкие звезды.

6. THE RETURN

A poem about Aleksey

It feels good to return:
to a city where everything's changed,
to a garden where years ago
some trees were cut down, and others
now creak, though they didn't used to,
to a home where they still mourn you.

To return and not say who you are.
To die having said not a thing.

And still they wrack their brains,
consult random passersby,
understand—but don't understand.

All the while things around you shine,
like faraway tiny stars.

7. ЖЕЛАНИЕ

Мало ли что мне казалось:
что если кого на свете хвалят,
то меня должны хвалить стократно,
а за что—пускай сами знают;

что нет такой злой минуты,
и такой забытой деревни,
и твари такой негодной,
что над нею дух не заиграет,
как чудесная дудка над кладом;

что нет среди смертей такой смерти,
чтобы силы у нее достало
против жизни моей терпеливой,
как полынь и сорные травы,—

мало ли что казалось
и что покажется дальше.

7. DESIRE

I used to think all kinds of things:
that if anyone on earth is praised,
I should be praised a hundred times more.
For what? That's not my problem.

That no moment is so evil
and no village so forgotten
and no critter so good-for-nothing
that the spirit won't play over it
like a magic flute with a treasure chest;

that amongst all deaths there's not a one
with the force that it would take
to undo this life of mine—
ah, it's patient as wormwood and weeds!

I used to think all kinds of things,
and I'll keep on thinking them yet.

8. ЗЕРКАЛО

Милый мой, сама не знаю:
к чему такое бывает?—

зеркальце вьется рядом
величиной с чечевицу
или как зерно просяное.

А что в нем горит и мнится,
смотрит, видится, сгорает,—
лучше совсем не видеть:

Жизнь ведь—небольшая вещица:
вся, бывает, соберется
на мизинце, на конце ресницы.
А смерть кругом нее, как море.

8. MIRROR

My darling, I don't know, either:
why do these things happen?—

there's a mirror that hangs beside us,
and the mirror's the size of a lentil
or of a grain of millet.

But what flares up and flashes in it,
what watches, what glimmers, what burns up there—
ah, those are things that shouldn't be seen:

I mean, life is such a small thing:
it can pull its whole self together
on your pinkie, on the tip of your eyelash.
And death surrounds it like the sea.

9. ВИДЕНИЕ

На тебя гляжу—и не тебя я вижу:
старого отца в чужой одежде.
Будто идти он не может,
а его всё гонят и гонят . . .

Господи, думаю, Боже,
или умру я скоро—
что это каждого жалко?

Зверей—за то, что они звери,
и воду—за то, что льется,
и злого—за его несчастье,
и себя—за свое безумье.

9. VISION

When I gaze at you—it's not you I see:
an aging father in someone else's clothes.
He looks like he can't even walk,
and still they chase him and they chase him . . .

God Almighty, I think,
I myself could die soon—
why am I sorry for every last one?

For the beasts—because they're beasts,
for the water—because it flows,
for the evil man—since he's unhappy,
and for myself—because I'm a fool.

10. ДОМ

Будем жить мы долго, так долго,
как живут у воды деревья,
как вода им корни умывает
и земля с ними к небу выходит,
Елизавета—к Марии.

Будем жить мы долго, долго.
Выстроим два высоких дома:
тот из золота, этот из мрака,
и оба шумят, как море.

Будут думать, что нас уже нет . . .
Тут-то мы им и скажем:

—По воде невидимой и быстрой
уплывает сердце человека.
Там летает ветхое время,
как голубь из Ноева века.

10. HOUSE

We'll live a long, long time, as long
as the trees live by the water,
as the water washes their roots
and earth goes off with them to heaven,
Elizabeth—to Mary.

We'll live a long, long time.
We'll build ourselves two tall houses:
one of gold and one of gloom,
and both will sound like the sea.

They'll think we're no longer there . . .
And then we'll say to them,

"Down water unseen and swift
a person's heart floats away.
There ancient time flies along
like the dove from the age of Noah."

11. СОН

Снится блудному сыну,
снится на смертном ложе,
как он уезжает из дома.

На нем веселое платье,
на руке прадедовский перстень.
Лошадь ему брат выводит.

Хорошо бывает рано утром:
за спиной гудят рожки и струны,
впереди еще лучше играют.

А собаки, слуги и служанки
у ворот собрались и смотрят,
желают счастливой дороги.

11. DREAM

The prodigal son is dreaming,
he's dreaming on his deathbed
that he is leaving home.

He's wearing a festive robe,
on his hand his great-grandfather's ring.
His brother brings him out his horse.

Early morning can be so lovely:
behind him horns and strings hum,
but they play even better up ahead.

And the dogs, the manservants and maidservants
all gather at the gate to see him off
and wish him happy trails.

12. ЗАКЛЮЧЕНИЕ

В каждой печальной вещи
есть перстень или записка,
как в условленных дуплах.

В каждом слове есть дорога,
путь унылый и страстный.

А тот, кто сказал, что может,
слёзы его не об этом,
и надежда у него другая.

Кто не знал ее—не узнает.
Кто знает—снова удивится,
снова в уме улыбнется
и похвалит милосердного Бога.

1981

12. CONCLUSION

In every single sad thing,
you'll find a ring or a note
like in the secret tree hollow.

In every word, you'll find a road,
a desolate path of passion.

And what you know is possible
is not what your tears are for,
and your hope lies in something else.

If you don't know it—you won't recognize it.
If you know it—it will astonish you yet.
And in your mind, you'll smile anew
and will praise the God of kindness.

1981

СТИХИ ИЗ ВТОРОЙ ТЕТРАДИ,
не нашедшие в ней себе места

ПИР

Кто умеет читать по звездам
или раскладывать камни,
песок варить и иголки,
чтобы узнать, что будет
из того, что бывает,—
тот еще знает не много.

Жизнь—как вино молодое.
Сколько его ни выпей,
ума оно не отнимет
и языка не развяжет.
Лучше не добивайся.

А как огни потушат
и все по домам разойдутся
или за столом задремлют,—
то-то страшно будет подумать,
где ты был и по какому делу,
с кем и о чем совещался.

POEMS FROM
THE SECOND NOTEBOOK
that couldn't find themselves a place there

FEAST

You may know how to read the stars,
or how to lay out stones,
or how to boil sand and needles
to discover what will be
out of everything that could be—
but you still don't know much.

Life is like young wine.
No matter how much you drink,
it won't rob you of your mind,
and it won't untie your tongue.
Don't waste your sweet time trying.

But when they've put the fires out,
and everyone's gone home
or has dozed off at the table—
oh, how terrible to think
where you were, what you were up to,
what you talked about and with whom.

ДРУГАЯ КОЛЫБЕЛЬНАЯ

Спи, голубчик, не то тебя бросят,
бросят и глядеть не будут,
как жница оставила сына
на краю ячменного поля.
Сама жнет и слезы утирает.

—Мама, мама, кто ко мне подходит,
кто это встал надо мною?

То стоят три чудные старухи,
то три седые волчицы.
Качают они, утешают,
нажуют они мелкого маку.
Маку ребенок не хочет,
плачет, а никто не слышит.

ANOTHER CRADLE SONG

Sleep, little dove, or they'll leave you behind,
leave you behind and not look back,
like a reaper who left her son
at the edge of the barley field.
And she reaps and wipes away her tears.

"Mama, mama, who comes this way,
who stands there over me now?"

Three wondrous old women stand there,
three grey-haired she-wolves stand there.
They rock him, and they lull him,
in their teeth, they grind poppy seeds.
He doesn't want the poppy, poor child,
he's crying, but no one hears.

СТАРУШКИ

Как старый терпеливый художник,
я люблю разглядывать лица
набожных и злых старушек:
смертные их губы
и бессмертную силу,
которая им губы сжала.

(Будто сидит там ангел,
столбцами складывает деньги:
пятаки и легкие копейки . . .
Кыш!—говорит он детям,
птицам и попрошайкам,—
кыш, говорит, отойдите:
не видите, что я занят?)

Гляжу—и в уме рисую:
как себя перед зеркалом темным.

OLD WOMEN

Like a patient old artist,
I love to look at the faces
of pious and spiteful old women:
at their mortal and venomous lips
and at the undying force
that has squeezed their lips tight shut.

(Imagine an angel sitting there
stacking up columns of money:
five-kopek coins and weightless kopeks . . .
"Shoo!" he says to the children,
to the birds and to the beggars,
"Shoo," he says, "go away:
can't you see how busy I am?")

I look—and draw him in my mind:
myself in a mirror darkly.

БУСЫ

Лазурный бабушкин перстень,
прадедовы книги—
это я отдам, быть может.
А стеклянные бусы
что-то мне слишком жалко.

Пестрые они, простые,
как сад и в саду павлины,
а их сердце из звезд и чешуек.

Или озеро, а в озере рыбы:
то черный вынырнет, то алый,
то кроткий, кроткий зеленый—
никогда он уже не вернется,
и зачем ему возвращаться!

Не люблю я бедных и богатых,
ни эту страну, ни другие,
ни время дня, ни время года—
а люблю, что мнится и винится:
таинственное веселье.
Ни цены ему нет, ни смысла.

BEADS

My grandmother's azure ring,
my great-grandfather's books—
those are things I might give away.
But for some reason, I'd regret
giving away the glass beads.

They're colorful, and they're simple
like a garden, and in the garden, peacocks,
but their heart is made of stars and scales.

Or a lake, and in the lake, some fish:
a black one swims up, then a scarlet one,
then the meekest, meekest green one—
it will never again return,
and why should it want to return!

I love neither poor nor rich,
not this country, nor the others,
not the time of day, nor the time of year—
but I love what is glimpsed and accused:
a mysterious revelry.
It has neither value nor meaning.

ПУТЕШЕСТВИЕ

Когда кончится это несчастье
или счастье это отвернется,
отойдет, как высокие волны,

я пойду по знакомой дороге
наконец-то, куда мне велели.

Буду тогда слушать, что услышу,
говорить, чтобы мне говорили:

—Вот, я ждал тебя—и дождался.
Знал всегда—и теперь узнаю.
Разве я что забуду?—

Каждый хочет, чтоб его узнали:
птицы бы к нему слетались,
умершие вставали живыми,
звери зверят приводили

и медленно катилось время,
как молния в раннем детстве.

JOURNEY

When at last this unhappiness ends
or this happiness turns away
and leaves me like tall waves,

I'll finally set off down that road
and go where I've been ordered.

Then I'll listen to what I'm told,
and I'll speak as to hear them say,

"I've been waiting for you—and here you are.
I've known you forever—and I know you now.
Did you really think I'd forget?"

Each one wants to be known:
for birds to fly down to him,
for the dead to rise up alive,
for the beasts to bring forth their young

and for time to roll slowly on
like lightning when you're very young.

ТРЕТЬЯ ТЕТРАДЬ

Памяти бабушки
Дарьи Семеновны Седаковой

1.

—Пойдем, пойдем, моя радость,
пойдем с тобой по нашему саду,
поглядим, что сделалось на свете!

Подай ты мне, голубчик, руку,
принеси мою старую клюшку.
Пойдем, а то лето проходит.

Ничего, что я лежу в могиле,—
чего человек не забудет!
Из сада видно мелкую реку.
В реке видно каждую рыбу.

THIRD NOTEBOOK (1982)

In memory of my grandmother
Darya Semyonova Sedakova

1.

"Let's go, let's go, joy of mine,
let's take a walk in our garden,
let's see what's been done in the world!

"Give me your hand, little dove,
bring me my old walking stick.
Let's go before summer is gone.

"It's one thing that I'm in my grave,--
but a person forgets all kinds of things!
From the garden, see, the shallow stream.
And in the stream, each fish."

2.

Что же я такое сотворила,
что свеча моя горит не ясно,
мигает, как глаза больные,
бессонные тусклые очи?—

Вспомню—много; забуду—еще больше.
Не хочу ни забывать, ни помнить.

Ах, много я на людей смотрела
и знаю странные вещи:
знаю, что душа—младенец,
младенец до последнего часа,

всему, всему она верит
и спит в разбойничьем вертепе.

2.

What, oh, what have I done?
Now my candle won't burn clearly,
it glimmers like ailing eyes,
like sleepless, clouded eyes—

There's much that I'll remember and more that I'll forget.
I don't want to forget or remember, either.

Ah, I've watched people a long, long time,
and strange things have I learned:
I know that the soul is an infant,
an infant until its final hour,

that it believes absolutely everything,
and it sleeps in a den of thieves.

3.

Женская доля—это прялка,
как на старых надгробьях,
и зимняя ночь без рассказов.

Росла сиротой, старела вдовой,
потом сама себе постыла.

Падала с неба золотая нитка,
падала, земли не достала.
Что же так сердце ноет?

Из глубины океана
выплывала чудесная рыба,
несла она жемчужный перстень,
до берега не доплыла.
Что в груди, как вьюга, воет?

Крикнуть бы—нечем крикнуть,
как жалко прекрасную землю!

3.

A woman's lot is the distaff,
as the ancient tombstones show,
and a winter's eve with no stories.

She grew up an orphan, grew old a widow,
and then grew sick of herself.

A golden needle fell from heaven;
it fell, but not all the way to earth.
Why does the heart moan so?

Up from the depths of the ocean
there swam a wondrous fish,
and it brought with it a pearl ring,
but it didn't make it to shore.
What howls in the breast like a blizzard?

If you could just cry—some way cry out
how sorry you feel for this splendid earth!

4.

Кто родится в черный понедельник,
тот уже о счастье не думай:
хорошо, если так обойдется
под твоей пропащей звездою.

Родилась я в черный понедельник
между Рождеством и Крещеньем,
когда ходит старая стужа,
как медведь на липовой ходуле:
—Кто там, дескать, вари́т мое мясо,
кто мою шерсть прядет-мотает?
и мигали мелкие звезды,
одна другой неизвестней.

И мне снилось, как меня любили
и ни в чем мне не было отказа,
гребнем золотым чесали косы,
на серебряных санках возили
и читали из таинственной книги
слова, какие я забыла.

4.

If you're born on a black Monday,
don't even think of happiness:
you'll do well just to get by
beneath your fallen star.

I was born on a black Monday
between Christmas and Epiphany,
when old frost roams about
like a bear on a linden stilt:
"Say, who there is boiling my meat,
who's spinning and winding my fleece?"
and the meager stars were blinking,
each one more unknown than the next.

And I dreamed that I was loved,
no request of mine was refused,
they combed my braids with a golden comb,
bore me on a golden sleigh
and read to me from a mysterious book
words, but what kind I've forgotten.

5.

Как из глубокого колодца
или со звезды далекой
смотрит бабушка из каждой вещи:

—Ничего, ничего мы не знаем.
Что видели, сказать не можем.

Ходим, как две побирушки.
Не дадут—и на том спасибо.

Про других мы ничего не знаем.

5.

From a deep well
as from a distant star,
my grandmother looks out from each thing:

"Nothing, we know nothing.
And what we've seen, we cannot say.

"We go around like two beggars.
We thank even those who don't give.

"For we know not a thing about anyone else."

6.

Были бы мастера на свете,
выстроили бы часовню
над нашим целебным колодцем
вместо той, какую здесь взорвали . . .

Было бы у меня усердье,
шила бы я тебе покровы:
или Николая Чудотворца,
или кого захочешь . . .

Подсказал бы мне ангел слово,
милое, как вечерние звезды,
дорогое для ума и слуха,
все бы его повторяли
и знали бы твою надежду . . . —

Ничего не надобно умершим,
ни дома, ни платья, ни слуха.
Ничего им от нас не надо.
Ничего, кроме всего на свете.

6.

Were there still skilled craftsmen on earth,
they would build us a chapel
over our wondrous healing well
where they blew up the other one . . .

And how industrious I would be,
I would sew you all kinds of covers:
ones with Nicholas the Wonderworker
or whomever else you like . . . .

An angel would bring me a word,
beloved as evening stars,
precious to mind and to ear alike,
and everyone would repeat it
and then they would know your hope . . .—

The dead don't need a thing,
not houses nor dresses nor hearing.
There's nothing they need from us.
Not a thing, save everything on earth.

7.

По дороге длинной, по дороге пыльной
шла я и горевала—
знаешь, как люди горюют?
Когда камень поплывет, как рыба,
тогда, говорю, и будет
для души моей жизнь и прощенье.

Поплывет себе камень, как лодка,
легкая при попутном ветре,
расправляя золотые ветрильца,
пестрые крапивницыны крылья,
золотыми веслами мелькая
по дальнему шумному морю.

И что было, того не будет.
Будет то, чего лучше не бывает.

7.

Down that long, down that dusty road
I walked, and I lamented—
do you know how people lament?
When a stone starts to swim like a fish,
that's when, I tell you, there will be
both life and forgiveness for this soul of mine.

A stone will set sail in itself like a boat,
light with a following wind,
spreading its golden sails,
its motley nettle-rash wings,
flashing its golden oars
down the distant, noisy sea.

And what has been, that is what will not be.
What will be is better than anything else.

8.

Ты гори, невидимое пламя,
ничего мне другого не нужно.
Все другое у меня отнимут.
Не отнимут, так добром попросят.
Не попросят, так сама я брошу,
потому что скучно и страшно.

Как звезда, глядящая на ясли,
или в чаще малая сторожка,
на цепях почерневших качаясь,
ты гори, невидимое пламя.

Ты лампада, слёзы твое масло,
жестокого сердца сомненье,
улыбка того, кто уходит.

Ты гори, передавай известье
Спасителю, небесному Богу,
что Его на земле еще помнят,
не всё еще забыли.

8.

Burn on, unseen flame,
there's nothing else I need.
Everything else they'll take from me.
What they don't take, they'll want me to offer.
What they don't want, I'll throw away,
for it's all so awful and frightening.

Like a star looking down on a manger
or a little lodge in the woods
swaying on blackened chains,
burn on, unseen flame.

You're an icon lamp, and your tears are of oil,
of the doubt in a hardened heart,
of the smile of someone departing.

Burn on, and send word
to our Savior, our heavenly God,
that He's still remembered on earth,
that they haven't forgotten everything yet.

9.

(Молитва)

Обогрей, Господь, Твоих любимых—
сирот, больных, погорельцев.

Сделай за того, кто не может,
всё, что ему велели.

И умершим, Господи, умершим—
пусть грехи их вспыхнут, как солома,
сгорят и следа не оставят
ни в могиле, ни в высоком небе.

Ты—Господь чудес и обещаний.
Пусть все, что не чудо, сгорает.

1982

9.

(Prayer)

Keep your beloved ones warm, oh Lord—
the orphans, the sick, the victims of fire.

Do for the one who can't
all that he's been told he must do.

And the dead, oh Lord, the dead—
may their sins blaze up like straw,
burn up and leave no trace
in the grave or in highest heaven.

You are Lord of wonders and promises.
May all but wonders burn up.

1982

ПРИБАВЛЕНИЯ К «СТАРЫМ ПЕСНЯМ»

ПОСВЯЩЕНИЕ

Помни, говорю я, помни,
помни, говорю и плачу:
все покинет, все переменится
и сама надежда убивает.

Океан не впадает в реку;
река не возвращается к истокам;
время никого не пощадило —

но я люблю тебя, как будто
все это было и бывает.

Additions to "Old Songs"

DEDICATION

Remember, say I, remember,
remember, I say, and weep:
all will abandon, all will be changed,
and hope is the thing that kills.

Ocean will never fall into river,
and river will never return to its source;
and there's not one soul that time has spared—

and yet I love you as if
all of that was and will be.

* * *

Плакал Адам, но его не простили.
И не позволили вернуться
туда, где мы только и живы:

—Хочешь своего, свое и получишь.
И что тебе делать такому
там, где сердце хочет, как Бог великий:
там, где сердце—сиянье и даренье.

* * *

Adam wept, but he wasn't forgiven.
And he was never allowed to return
to the only place we're really alive:

"You want what's yours? You can have it.
And what's there to do for one such as you
where what the heart wants is great as God:
where the heart is all radiance and offering."

* * *

Холод мира
кто-нибудь согреет.

Мертвое сердце
кто-нибудь поднимет.

Этих чудищ
кто-нибудь возьмет за руку,
как ошалевшего ребенка:

—Пойдем, я покажу тебе такое,
чего ты никогда не видел!

1990-1992

* * *

Someone will warm
the cold of the world.

Someone will raise up
the dead heart.

Someone will take
these beasts by the hand
like an unruly child:

"Come with me, I'll show you something
the likes of which you've never seen!"

1990-1992

Acknowledgments

USUALLY WE ACKNOWLEDGE the most important person last. But pride of place in this list goes to Olga Sedakova. Olga Aleksandrovna manifests the generosity and sensibility her poems voice; she has encouraged and offered concrete support to my translation and scholarly efforts since I first shared them with her. I hear in these poems her wry, warm tones, and I spy in them the lush summer gardens at her rural Azarovka village home.

Several poems from this collection have been published elsewhere. "Beads" appears courtesy of *Poetry Daily* and also by courtesy of Two Lines Press, who included it in their anthology *vot my so scheta sbilis'/ This Is Us Losing Count: Eight Russian Poets* (2022). "Desire" is also included in this anthology.

In many ways my journey translating Sedakova began with a request to translate her for a volume of scholarly essays. "Sin," "Journey," "From a deep well," "Someone will warm," "Adam wept, but he wasn't forgiven," "Let's go, let's go, joy of mine," "Childhood," "There's a man who is spiteful and mean," "The Unfaithful Wife," and "Consolation" appeared in part or in whole in *The Poetry and Poetics of Olga Sedakova*, edited by Stephanie Sandler, Maria Khotimsky, Margarita Krimmel, and Oleg Novikov (University of Wisconsin Press, 2017). So these poems appear by courtesy of University of Wisconsin Press. I am grateful to these extraordinary editors for the opportunity to grow as a translator, and for their guidance. (Stephanie Sandler is a revered translator in her own right and Maria Khotimsky a cutting-edge scholar of translation.) Their volume, by the way, is the best place to start for those wanting to read more about Sedakova in English.

Thanks go to the National Humanities Center, a place of magic and trees; and to the Mellon Foundation for funding my fellowship. I'm not sure I could have wrapped this project up anywhere else. Many thanks also to Greg Wolfe and his team at Slant for calling this project out of its digital existence and into a shareable and more refined form. And heartfelt thanks to Gabe, my wisest, kindest reader.

This book was set in Garamond Premier Pro, designed by Robert Slimbach and published in 1989. It had its genesis in 1988 when Adobe senior type designer Robert Slimbach visited the Plantin-Moretus Museum in Antwerp, Belgium, to study their collection of Claude Garamond's metal punches and type designs.

This book was designed by Shannon Carter, Ian Creeger, and Gregory Wolfe. It was published in hardcover, paperback, and electronic formats by Slant Books, Seattle, Washington.

Cover: *Balalaika*, by Thorvald Hellesen. Circa 1914-1916. Courtesy of Nasjonalmuseet, Olso.